DATE D0118945

NOV 07 2008

PRINTED IN U.S.A.

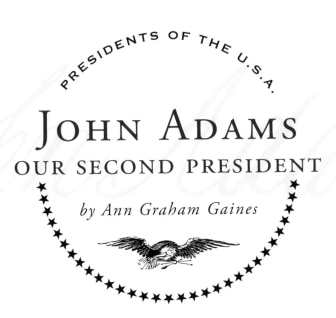

PRESIDENTS OF THE U.S.A.

JOHN ADAMS
OUR SECOND PRESIDENT

by Ann Graham Gaines

THE CHILD'S WORLD®

Published in the United States of America

The Child's World®
1980 Lookout Drive • Mankato, MN 56003-1705
800-599-READ • www.childsworld.com

Acknowledgments
The Child's World®: Mary Berendes, Publishing Director

The Creative Spark: Mary McGavic, Project Director; Shari Joffe, Editorial
Director; Deborah Goodsite, Photo Research; Nancy Ratkiewich, Page Production

The Design Lab: Kathleen Petelinsek, Design

Content Adviser: Caroline Keinath, Deputy Superintendent, Adams National
Historical Park, Quincy, Massachusetts

Photos
Cover and page 3: National Park Service, Adams National Historical Park

Interior: Adams Family Papers, Massachusetts Historical Society: 13 inset;
The Bridgeman Art Library International: 4, 9 (Massachusetts Historical
Society, Boston, MA), 17 (Hall of Representatives, Washington D.C.), 24
(Collection of the New-York Historical Society); 28 (Archives du Ministere des
Affaires Etrangeres, Paris, France, Archives Charmet), 30 (Library of Congress,
Washington D.C.), 32 (Peabody Essex Museum, Salem, Massachusetts), 37
bottom (Collection of the New-York Historical Society); Corbis: 7, 16 (Bettmann/
CORBIS); Getty Images: 12, 31 (MPI), 13 (Andreas Feininger/Time & Life
Pictures); iStockphoto: 44 (Tim Fan); National Park Service, Adams National
Historical Park: 5 and 38 top, 14, 15, 19 top, 19 bottom, 21 and 39 left, 23, 34;
North Wind Picture Archives: 20 (North Wind); Stock Montage; SuperStock,
Inc.: 8 and 38 bottom (Library of Congress, Washington D.C.), 10, 11 (Yale
University Art Gallery, New Haven, CT, USA), 27 and 39 right (SuperStock), 33
(Huntington Library, Art Collections, and Botanical Gardens, San Marino, CA);
U.S. Air Force photo: 45.

Library of Congress Cataloging-in-Publication Data
Gaines, Ann.
  John Adams / by Ann Graham Gaines.
      p. cm.—(Presidents of the U.S.A.)
  Includes bibliographical references and index.
   ISBN 978-1-60253-031-7 (library bound : alk. paper)
  1. Adams, John, 1735–1826—Juvenile literature. 2. Presidents—United
States—Biography—Juvenile literature. I. Title.
  E322.G18 2008
  973.4'4'092—dc21
  [B]
                              2007042601

John Adams, one of the founding fathers of the United States, was an independent thinker and a passionate patriot.

TABLE OF CONTENTS

AMERICAN PATRIOT

John Adams was the second president of the United States. He had a very difficult job to do. As a young man, he was a patriot who helped convince Americans to fight for independence from Great Britain and found a new nation. When he became president 22 years later, his most important job was to help the nation survive. To do so, he had to keep the United States out of a war with France.

John Adams was born on October 30, 1735, in Braintree, Massachusetts (a small town 12 miles from Boston). His parents owned a farm. Their rocky land was hilly, but they managed to raise good crops. Adams's father was an important man in Braintree. He was a church **deacon** and a member of the town council.

John Adams was a young, newly married lawyer when Benjamin Blyth painted this portrait in 1766.

Adams's mother and father read all the time. At a young age, John began to love books as well. He knew how to read by the time he went to a dame school

that was similar to kindergarten. He liked it there, but he soon got old enough to go to the town's public school. His new teacher did not pay enough attention to his students. Adams later said this made him dislike going to school. He was happier outside, where he and his two brothers played marbles, wrestled, swam, and skated. He made toy boats to sail and kites to fly.

For a while, John Adams thought he wanted to grow up to become a farmer like his father. He saw no reason to go to college. Then, when he was 14, his father sent him to a **tutor.** Adams studied so hard that he was ready to go to Harvard College in just one year. At the time, there were just a few colleges in the American colonies, and Harvard was the best.

John Adams was born on his parents' farm, shown in the painting above, in Braintree, Massachusetts. His father's family had lived in Massachusetts for generations.

The Adamses had a large, extended family in Braintree. They lived close to grandparents, aunts, uncles, and cousins. Members of the family had been living in Braintree for more than 100 years.

John Adams learned to shoot a gun when he was still a small boy. He sometimes skipped school so he could hunt ducks in the marshes near his house.

Going there almost guaranteed success in life. Adams graduated from Harvard in 1755. He was one of the best students in his class.

While in college, Adams decided to become a lawyer. There were no law schools in those days. Students paid lawyers to tutor them in their offices. Adams moved to the town of Worcester to become a teacher. He used the money he earned to pay his tutor.

Adams made many friends. A deep thinker as well as a lover of books, he liked to talk about **politics** with them. But other people's ideas rarely influenced him. All his life, Adams had an independent mind.

In 1756, at age 21, Adams had earned enough money to pay for lessons in law. In two years, he opened his own law office in Braintree. Later he had an office in Boston, the capital of the Massachusetts Colony.

Boston was a big town with a harbor that was always filled with ships. Adams was amazed by how busy it was. Its streets were filled with "Chimney Sweeps, Carriers of Wood, Merchants, Ladies, Priests, Carts, Horses, Oxen, Coaches, Market men and women, Soldiers, Sailors." There was so much noise that sometimes he found it difficult to think.

As a lawyer, his work took him to courts all over Massachusetts. He earned a reputation for being smart and for winning arguments. He also became known for his quick temper.

In 1761, Adams's father died, leaving him a house in Braintree as an **inheritance.** In 1764, John

Adams married Abigail Smith. They soon started to raise a family.

Over the years, Adams became even more interested in politics. He began to write articles and books on the subject, focusing on the rights of Great Britain's American colonies. He believed that the colonists were not represented in the British government. People read everything he wrote.

Harvard College was established in 1636. Today known as Harvard University, it is the oldest college in the United States. When John Adams entered Harvard in 1751, he became the first in his family to go to college.

He became a **spokesperson** for the patriots, the colonists who thought the colonies should break away from England.

England had begun to pass laws that said colonists had to pay taxes. English officials collected these taxes from the colonists and sent them to the king of England. In 1765, John Adams's career was hurt by the passage of the Stamp Act. This act said that all documents must carry a stamp bought from the British government. When the people of Massachusetts refused to buy these stamps, the government shut down the colony's courts. For a time, Adams had no work. He spent his time writing a book and articles that showed why the Stamp Act was unfair. Eventually, the Act was repealed.

In 1770, John Adams started a new career when he was elected to the Massachusetts **legislature.** For a long time, he hoped the patriots would not have to fight to win independence for the colonies. But in December 1773, colonists protested new taxes placed on tea. They disguised themselves as Indians and boarded British ships carrying tea that had docked in Boston's harbor. Then they dumped all the tea into the water. It was ruined and could not be sold. England would earn no taxes from it. This protest became known as the Boston

John Adams called his wife, Abigail, his best friend.

Tea Party. Adams described it as "the grandest event which has ever yet happened."

The angry British government closed the harbor at Boston, letting no ships sail in or out. This left the town short of supplies, which Adams thought was unfair. He became convinced a **revolution** was coming. He committed himself to leading the patriots, saying he would "live or die, survive or perish with my country." From this point on, Adams encouraged other people

In 1773, colonists protesting British taxes dressed up as American Indians, boarded three British ships, and dumped more than 300 chests of tea overboard. John Adams, like other patriots, celebrated this event.

Benjamin Franklin, John Adams, and Thomas Jefferson (from left to right) were all on the committee that Congress charged with writing the Declaration of Independence. Although Jefferson actually wrote this important document, Adams and Franklin gave him advice and support.

It was John Adams who suggested to the Continental Congress that the colonies needed to form a single army—and that George Washington should be chosen to lead it.

from Massachusetts to accept the fact that they were going to have to fight for their freedom.

In 1774, the people of Massachusetts elected John Adams to the First **Continental Congress.** This group of **representatives** from all thirteen colonies met in

Philadelphia to discuss how to deal with Great Britain. The people of Massachusetts thought Adams did a very good job there, so they elected him to the Second Continental Congress as well. He served on many different committees. In 1776, his friends in Congress asked him to be in charge of the committee that would write the Declaration of Independence. The committee of five discussed what the Declaration should say, and then Thomas Jefferson wrote it. When the Congress finally approved the Declaration on July 4, 1776, the United States was born.

John Adams was one of the signers of the Declaration of Independence. In this famous painting by John Trumbull, Adams is the first man standing on the left.

THE BOSTON MASSACRE

On March 5, 1770, British soldiers fired into a crowd and killed five colonists in Boston. Samuel Adams, John Adams's cousin, immediately called the event the "Boston Massacre." Sam Adams asked Paul Revere to create a picture of it, and copies were sent all over the colonies. Revere's picture is shown above. Learning about the Boston Massacre stirred up patriotic feelings among the colonists.

John Adams, however, believed that both the British and the Americans were to blame for the massacre. He considered the deaths tragic, but he also thought the American mob had behaved badly. As a lawyer, he even defended the British soldiers in court. All but two of these soldiers were found innocent. This is an example of what an independent thinker Adams was. He was a patriot, yet he helped the English soldiers who he thought were being treated unfairly.

JOHN ADAMS'S WRITINGS

Throughout his life, John Adams was a very prolific writer, meaning he wrote an enormous amount. As a lawyer and politician, he wrote many legal documents, as well as articles and books about government. In his free time, he also wrote thousands of letters. Many of them were to his beloved wife, Abigail. They constantly corresponded, writing not just about their family, but about what was happening in the world.

　　John Adams's family saved his writings. Today most of them are housed at the Massachusetts Historical Society. Historians see them as extremely interesting and use them to find out about life during the American Revolution and the early days of the United States.

John Adams's writing desk (at left) at his home in Quincy

CHAPTER TWO

A WEAK VICE PRESIDENT

In 1777, the Second Continental Congress asked John Adams to take on a new role, as a **diplomat.** The new nation, at war with Great Britain, needed to establish relations with other European countries. John Adams's new assignment meant he had to leave his wife and young children and go overseas, first to France and then to Holland.

Before Adams left for Europe, he bought this locket for Abigail. It features a painting of a woman gazing sadly at a ship headed out to sea. Adams thought it would symbolize the pain his wife felt at his departure.

John Adams made a good diplomat. He worked hard explain-ing to European kings and officials why Americans wanted and deserved their independence. In 1778, he helped convince France to fight with the United States in the Revolution, which greatly strengthened American forces. In 1779, he came home for a short time. Back in Massachusetts, he drew on his

legal training and wrote a new **constitution** for the state of Massachusetts, one of the most successful ever written. Soon afterward, he returned to Europe with his oldest son, John Quincy Adams, who also had a career as a diplomat. In 1780, John Adams convinced Holland to lend the United States money it desperately needed to go on fighting its war for independence.

By 1781, the British were tired of what was turning out to be a long and expensive war. The British general, Charles Cornwallis, **surrendered** to American general George Washington. The American Revolution was over, although it took two years for the United States and England to sign a peace **treaty.** John Adams **negotiated** the Treaty of Paris. He then became the U.S. **minister** to Great Britain. Finally,

Adams helped negotiate the Treaty of Paris, which ended the Revolutionary War. The American diplomats involved in the treaty were (from left to right) John Jay, John Adams, Benjamin Franklin, Henry Laurens, and William Temple Franklin. The British commissioners refused to pose, so the painting was never finished.

When John Adams was a diplomat in Europe, he made many important decisions without consulting U.S. leaders. To ask Congress what to do would have taken too long. It took many weeks for a letter and its response to go back and forth across the ocean.

after many years of separation, his wife and daughter came to live with him.

After the Revolution ended, American leaders had time to discuss exactly what form of government the new nation needed. In 1787, a book that Adams wrote about constitutions was published. Representatives at the **Constitutional Convention** read both Adams's book and the Massachusetts Constitution. His words guided them as they decided what to include in the U.S. Constitution. His ideas helped shape the American government.

In 1785, John Adams became the first U.S. minister to Great Britain. This engraving shows him making a presentation to King George III of England.

John Adams always wanted the new nation to establish a **democracy.** He once wrote that he was a firm "enemy to **monarchy,**" countries such as England that were ruled by a king or queen. In a democracy, citizens have freedom of speech, and Adams worked hard to make sure that Americans could openly express their opinions. On the other hand, a democracy should allow all its citizens the right to vote. Adams did not think that everyone should have that right. He believed only people with money and education should be allowed to vote. Adams paid close attention as the Constitutional Convention determined such matters, although he was still thousands of miles away in England.

Adams was not involved in the creation of the U.S. Constitution, but his ideas did influence its writers. Adams liked the role he played in the process. He recognized that few people have the great honor and responsibility of founding a new government.

One reason George Washington wanted John Adams to be his vice president was that Adams was from the North, while he was from the South. Washington wanted to make sure that all Americans felt represented in the new government.

John Adams administered the oath of office to George Washington at his **inauguration** on April 30, 1789.

In 1788, John Adams and his family returned to the United States. Crowds turned out to meet them. The Massachusetts legislature sent him an official notice saying how pleased the colony was to have Adams and his family safely back in Massachusetts. It also recognized his hard work.

He retired to Braintree to farm. A year later he agreed to run in the first presidential election ever held in the United States, even though he, like other Americans, expected—and wanted—George Washington to win. The **Electoral College** did in fact cast the most votes for George Washington. John Adams came in second, which in the early years of the nation meant he became the vice president.

Although being elected vice president excited him at first, Adams did not like his new job. George Washington did not consider Adams his assistant. He believed the vice president's job was simply to **preside** over the Senate. Adams attended and ran Senate sessions. At first, he also participated in Senate debates. But after he irritated the senators by pushing them to require that George Washington be addressed as "Your Highness," they decided the vice president could no longer speak. His job was then limited to casting tie-breaking votes. Although he was not a senator, he voted to break a tie many times when the senators could not agree on whether a **bill** should become law. This did not satisfy him. A smart man who was used to having people listen to him, Adams was unhappy. Sometimes he became angry when people did not share his point of view. He thought people were fools to disagree with him. Adams complained that the vice presidency was "the most insignificant office" that any person had ever held.

Both Adams and Abigail experienced great unhappiness during this time. At first, she lived with him in New York, the capital city at the time. But she later went back to live in Quincy (Braintree's new name). She and John had found it too expensive to live in New York because they were expected to have many parties with expensive food and wine. They missed each other terribly, but John Adams believed he still had a duty to serve the nation. He agreed to a second term as vice president.

John Adams was never very happy as George Washington's vice president. Nevertheless, he and Abigail always felt great affection and respect for both George and Martha Washington. In fact, they regarded them so highly that Adams had these portraits of the Washingtons painted. Adams hung them in his dining room.

Adams described himself during the vice presidency as "a mere mechanical tool to wind up the clock." He was pleased when his time in that office was over.

In 1796, George Washington refused to run for president a third time. John Adams agreed to run for the office, and he hoped he would be elected. When he was vice president, he once wrote, "I am weary of the game [of politics], yet I don't know how I could live out of it." A proud man, he also believed he would do well. He did not realize how important it is for a president to get along with other people.

ABIGAIL ADAMS

John Adams depended on his wife throughout their 54-year marriage. Born Abigail Smith, she was the daughter of a minister. Hers was a cultured and important family. She had no more education than other women of her day, but she was intelligent and interested in ideas. When Adams went to Europe as a diplomat, Abigail remained home for a long time. During most of the Revolution, she and their children lived on their farm at Quincy. She supported the family by running the farm. After the war ended, she and their daughter sailed to England to be with John, where Abigail charmed British leaders and made her husband's job much easier. She later played an important public role back in the United States as well.

Today Abigail Adams continues to inspire American women. Devoted to her husband and her family, she also cared about the issues of the day. She was one of the first Americans who spoke about women's rights. She was unhappy that women had few opportunities. For one thing, she believed women had a right to an education. In a famous letter to John Adams, written in March 1776, she told him to "remember the ladies" as he helped craft the policies of what would soon be a new nation. "Do not put such unlimited power into the hands of the Husbands," wrote Abigail.

CHAPTER THREE

THE PRESIDENCY

When George Washington was elected president for the first time in 1789, **political parties** did not yet exist in the United States. During his presidency, politicians broke into two groups. **Federalists** believed that the nation needed a very strong central government. **Democratic-Republicans** thought states should keep a lot of power. John Adams, like Washington, did not like the creation of these political parties. He thought that these groups would make it more difficult for politicians to cooperate and get things done. They would be too busy arguing with people from other political parties who had ideas different from their own.

By the late 1790s, however, politicians needed the support of a party to win an election. So Adams let the Federalist Party **nominate** him. The Republican Party nominated Thomas Jefferson. When the electoral votes were counted, Adams had received 71 and Jefferson had received 68. Adams had just barely won. Thomas Jefferson became his vice president even though he belonged to a different political party. All through Adams's term, he and Jefferson, once friends, would

This portrait features Adams in the suit he wore to his inauguration. Although his presidency would be a troubled one, Adams managed to keep the new government stable by keeping many of Washington's policies.

One reason Americans believed John Adams would make a good president was that he was an excellent diplomat.

argue over decisions that had to be made, especially about how to deal with the country of France.

John Adams's inauguration took place in 1797. At the ceremony, Washington, who was about to retire,

Alexander Hamilton (right) and John Adams both belonged to the Federalist Party, but they did not get along. Hamilton wanted his ideas to influence the president, but Adams—always an independent thinker—would not listen to him.

received more attention than Adams, but Adams did not seem to mind. Adams did not have very much experience in running a government. But he was used to working hard and he set right to it. Having no secretary, he handled all his own paperwork, reviewing reports and writing letters.

One thing Adams did not have to do was choose a **cabinet.** He simply kept the cabinet members George Washington had chosen. This later became a problem. At the end of his presidency, George Washington had often taken the advice of Alexander Hamilton.

Although Hamilton left Washington's cabinet, he still influenced his former coworkers. He was also the leader of the Federalist Party. Despite the fact that they shared some views, Hamilton and Adams disliked each other and found it very difficult to work together.

Hamilton expected to influence Adams because they belonged to the same political party. But Adams did not want anyone's advice. He believed that Americans expected the man they elected president to think for himself. This made Hamilton angry. Adams grew angry as well when he began to see that the cabinet was more loyal to Hamilton than to him.

Foreign affairs took up most of Adams's time while he was president. After the American Revolution, England and France both treated the United States poorly. After a time, the situation with England improved. The situation with France, on the other hand, did not. Nearly a decade before, in 1789, a violent revolution had erupted in France. That country's king was replaced with a new government, which declared that France would overthrow other countries' monarchies as well.

Then, in 1793, France declared war on Spain and Great Britain. The French expected Americans to fight with them. Earlier, the United States and France had signed a treaty that said the United States would join France if it ever went to war. Most Americans did not want to keep this promise. In fact, President Washington declared the United States **neutral.**

John Adams was the first president to live in the White House.

July 4 became Independence Day because that was the day Congress had voted in favor of the Declaration of Independence. John Adams always believed that Independence Day should have been on July 2, the day Congress had voted in favor of becoming independent from England. But by the time Adams became president, Americans were already celebrating the holiday on July 4.

Many Americans did not want the United States to fight for France. They did not think the French had the right to overthrow other peoples' governments. But some Americans thought the United States owed loyalty to France because it had helped them win the American Revolution.

By the time Adams became president in 1797, the French had decided they wanted nothing to do with the United States. They ordered an American diplomat to leave France. They also stopped trading goods with the United States. At sea, French ships attacked American ships.

In 1797, Adams sent American officials to talk to the French about these problems. Unfortunately, French leaders refused to see the Americans unless they paid a **bribe.** They also demanded that the American government lend France a huge amount of money. The American officials sent messages to Adams telling him what had happened. In these letters, they referred to the French leaders not by their real names, but by the letters X, Y, and Z.

President Adams refused to pay France the money it wanted. He went to Congress to tell his fellow politicians about the "XYZ Affair." Adams asked Congress to get ready to fight the French, but not actually to declare war. The public supported Adams.

In 1798, it looked as if war would soon break out between the United States and France. Adams ordered new ships to be built for the American navy. He asked George Washington to serve as commander

in chief of the army. This meant Washington took a position that should be the president's, according to the Constitution. But Adams believed Washington could do a better job.

Many Americans began to fear that foreigners might try to destroy the American government. A French general had already come to North America

The creation of the United States led some Europeans to question whether monarchs had the overall right to rule people. By 1789, the citizens of France had begun their own revolution, as shown above.

French officials demanded $250,000 before they would even listen to the Americans who had come to fix problems between the two countries. Here France is shown as a five-headed monster demanding money from U.S. representatives.

and tried to set up another new nation to the west of the United States. Many Americans considered this a serious threat.

To keep the United States safe, Congress passed the **Alien** and **Sedition** Acts. There were three Alien Acts, two of which could be used to make aliens—foreigners—leave the country—even if they had done nothing wrong. A third act increased the length of time it took for **immigrants** to become U.S. citizens. The

Sedition Act said that no one, whether an American or a foreigner, could say anything bad about the government or its leaders.

Adams had not asked for these acts to be passed. In fact, he did not want them, but he did sign them into law. Some important leaders thought this was a terrible mistake. They pointed out, for one thing, that the Sedition Act took away Americans' freedom of speech. The laws expired in 1801. Today historians agree that the laws were dangerous.

When Adams moved into the White House, fires were lit in each of the mansion's 39 fireplaces. The plaster walls were still wet, and builders hoped the fires would help to dry them.

In this 1798 cartoon, the Federalists and Republicans in Congress are shown fighting about the Alien and Sedition Acts. Federalists believed the acts would prevent enemies from hurting the United States. Republicans believed the new laws denied the rights guaranteed by the Constitution.

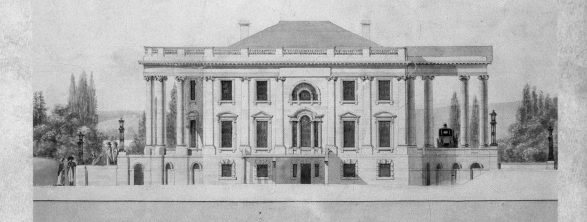

THE WHITE HOUSE

Today Washington, D.C., is the capital city of the United States, but it did not even exist when John Adams was elected vice president. First the capital was in New York. Later it was moved to Philadelphia. Soon government leaders decided to build a brand new capital city. The first public buildings that went up were the Capitol and the president's mansion.

When the Adamses arrived in Washington, D.C., the city was still being built. There were fields and swamps in the center of town. John and Abigail Adams became the first residents of the president's mansion on November 1, 1800. It wasn't until President James Monroe's term that people began calling the mansion the White House.

The president's mansion was very large. Eventually, it would be elegant, but it was still unfinished during John Adams's time. Abigail Adams described it as a castle but noted that it sat amid what was still a wild landscape. She wrote to a friend that she had ridden into town on a dirt path. In town, carriages got stuck in muddy streets, and people had to climb out and walk the rest of the way. When she arrived in the city, there was not yet a library or even a church.

CHAPTER FOUR

SAVING THE NATION FROM WAR

Early in his presidency, John Adams achieved success. Today most Americans don't realize that people wondered whether the nation would survive without George Washington as president. Some worried that the country would not prove strong enough to remain independent; others thought the states might not be able to cooperate and stay united. Even though John Adams was not popular, he did manage to keep the country in one piece.

By the time Adams became president, Great Britain no longer threatened American independence, as it had once done. But the young nation faced another

During Adams's presidency, France—not England—was America's enemy.

From 1798 through 1800, U.S. ships battled the French navy, although the two nations were never actually at war. This painting shows an American ship trying to outrun a French fleet.

For a time during his presidency, John Adams felt so much under attack in the capital that he went home to Quincy. He stayed there for eight months.

threat, this time from France, its former ally. France was under the rule of a government determined to expand its empire, taking over other countries. The French navy continued to try to capture American ships to seize their valuable cargo.

From 1798 to 1800, American vessels fought the French in an undeclared war at sea. By this time, Adams began to think his most important job was to work for peace. He found himself practically alone in this opinion, however. Adams was a stubborn man, and he had never learned to compromise. He had failed to form many political friendships. Still, he remained committed to his ideals.

Most of all, Adams wanted the United States to grow and prosper. He was afraid that war would hurt the new country too much, perhaps even causing it to fall apart. He worked on a peace plan all by himself. Finally, he sent a peace mission to France. William Vans Murray worked out an agreement with Charles Tallyrand, France's foreign minister. Together they drew up the Convention of 1800. This treaty succeeded in stopping the battles at sea and ended the threat of war with France. The Senate voted in favor of the treaty, even though many Americans—supporters of Alexander Hamilton—did not like it. They believed the country should have gone to war against France. Adams was accused of being unfit to serve as president. The situation upset him.

Even while under attack, Adams did his job. In 1800, the **federal** government moved to Washington, D.C., the nation's new capital city. John Adams moved into what Americans now call the White House, becoming the first president to live there. Abigail soon arrived, too.

Adams ran for a second term as president, again as a Federalist. But the Democratic-Republicans won, which meant that Thomas Jefferson was elected president. Adams's feelings were hurt. He believed Americans did not understand all he had done for them. Late in his life he wrote, "I never engaged in public affairs for my own interest, pleasure, envy . . . or even the desire of fame."

The very day Jefferson was sworn in as the third president of the United States, Adams left Washington. He was glad to return to Quincy. Earlier, he had

In 1848, Charles Francis Adams published a book featuring his grandmother Abigail's letters. It was the first book ever published about a first lady.

written to Abigail of his feeling that he would never have a place of his own: "Oh! that I could have a home! But this felicity has never been permitted me."

In Quincy, he enjoyed working on his farm and visiting neighbors. He continued to write and receive

Thomas Jefferson (right) and Adams had been close friends during the Revolution, but their opposing ideas separated them as the new nation took shape. The election of 1800 saw Adams and Jefferson running against each other again. But this time, Jefferson would win.

many letters, just as he had all his life. He read a great deal and enjoyed spending time with his children, grandchildren, and great-grandchildren who lived close to him.

For a long time after retiring, John Adams stayed active. Toward the very end, however, he began to look and feel old. He could no longer see or hear well, but his mind stayed clear. Over time, Americans seem to have forgotten anger they may have felt towards him. He became regarded as a wise man, to whom the nation owed thanks.

After he lost the election of 1800, John Adams returned to Massachusetts. He and Abigail moved into a house they had purchased 12 years before. The house is known today as "Old House," and it is still in existence.

John Adams and John Quincy Adams were the first father and son to both serve as the U.S. president. It took 175 years for this to happen again. George W. Bush, son of George Bush, became the 43rd president of the United States in 2001. His father was the 41st president.

When John Adams lost his eyesight, his family read books and letters to him. Reading was always one of his passions.

On October 28, 1818, Abigail Adams died, to her husband's great sorrow. They had been married for 54 years. In 1825, Adams's son, John Quincy Adams, became the sixth president of the United States. The new president immediately sat down and wrote to his father in Quincy. John Adams replied, "The multitude of my thoughts, and the intensity of my feelings are too much." In private, he said to a neighbor, "No man who ever held the office of president would congratulate a friend on obtaining it."

In 1826, the United States celebrated its 50th birthday. The people of Quincy wanted John Adams to appear at the town's celebration. By this time, he was 90 years old. His health was so bad that he spent his days in bed, and he could not attend the celebration. A small group of town leaders visited Adams at his home to ask for a toast for the celebration. Adams responded, "I will give you Independence Forever." When they asked if he would like to add anything more, he replied, "Not a word." In a matter of days, he died—on July 4, 1826, the very day the nation was prepared to celebrate its 50th anniversary.

The nation was filled with sorrow over the loss of one of its founding fathers, a man who dedicated his life to his country. Many people had complained about President Adams while he was in office, but what Americans remembered of him in the end was that he had helped the United States win—and keep—its independence.

FRIENDSHIP

When John Adams (top) and Thomas Jefferson
(bottom) were appointed to the committee to
create the Declaration of Independence,
they scarcely knew each other. Adams
had seen Jefferson in Congress,
but "I never heard him utter three
sentences together," he wrote
in his autobiography. Still, he
knew that Jefferson had the
reputation of being a fine writer.
Later in life, Adams said the
committee wanted him and
Jefferson to write the Declaration,
but he insisted Jefferson take
on the task because he was more
popular and a better writer.

 In 1784, he and Jefferson worked
together after Adams went to Europe to help
negotiate business treaties. They remained friends,
but they held different views concerning
the degree to which Americans could
govern themselves. Soon they began
to argue. In 1796, Thomas Jefferson
was elected John Adams's vice
president. They remained at
odds. In 1800, Adams was angry
and disappointed when he lost
the presidential election to
Jefferson, and their friendship
suffered further. They rekindled
their friendship in 1812 through
letters, which continued the rest
of their days. Amazingly, both John
Adams and Thomas Jefferson died
on July 4, 1826. Both had been ill but
wanted to live until the 50th anniversary
of the Declaration of Independence.

| 1730 | 1750 | 1760 | 1770 | |

1735
John Adams is born on October 30 in Braintree, Massachusetts. His parents, John Adams and Suzanna Boylston Adams, own a small farm.

1751
Fifteen-year-old John Adams begins taking classes at Harvard College.

1755
Adams graduates from Harvard. He becomes a teacher for a short time to help pay for a law tutor.

1756
Adams starts to study law with a tutor named James Putnam.

1758
Adams opens his own law office. He argues cases all over the Massachusetts colony.

1761
Adams's father dies. John Adams inherits a house and farm in Braintree, where he was born.

1764
Adams marries Abigail Smith. They will have six children, five of whom will live to adulthood.

1765
Adams, now a patriot, believes that England is violating colonists' rights.

1770
Adams is elected to the state legislature. The Boston Massacre takes place in March. Although Adams is committed to American independence, he defends the British soldiers involved in the attack, believing that he must uphold the law.

1773
The Boston Tea Party takes place on December 16.

1774
Adams closes his law office when he is elected to the First Continental Congress. Delegates from all the colonies meet in Philadelphia.

1776
As a member of the Second Continental Congress, Adams is named to the committee asked to write the Declaration of Independence. This will be a statement in which the former colonies say they are no longer part of England.

1777
Congress asks Adams to become a diplomat. He agrees to travel to France and Holland as a representative of the United States.

1779
Adams writes a new constitution for Massachusetts.

1780
As a diplomat, Adams makes arrangements for his country to borrow a large amount of money from Holland.

1783
Adams helps negotiate the Treaty of Paris, officially ending the Revolutionary War.

1784
Abigail Adams joins John Adams in London after years of separations.

1785
Adams becomes the first American diplomat received by the king of England.

1787
A book about constitutions, written by Adams, is published. The Constitutional Convention will use the book to help create the U.S. Constitution.

1788
After more than 10 years of working as a diplomat in Europe, Adams finally returns to the United States.

1789
Adams places second in the first U.S. presidential election, which makes him vice president. George Washington is president.

1793
George Washington and John Adams are both reelected.

1797
John Adams is inaugurated as the second president of the United States. Thomas Jefferson is his vice president. After continued problems between France and the United States, Adams sends U.S. officials to try to improve relations. The French refuse to see the American officials unless they receive money in return. The event is called the XYZ Affair.

1798
The United States begins to fight the French at sea, but the countries never declare war. Congress passes the Alien and Sedition Acts, which are supposed to keep foreigners from making trouble in the United States. The Sedition Act also makes it illegal for Americans to complain in public about the government.

1800
The federal government moves to Washington, D.C. Adams becomes the first president to live in the White House. Diplomats that Adams has sent to France finally negotiate peace. He leaves office after losing the presidential election to Thomas Jefferson and returns to Quincy.

1801
The Alien and Sedition Acts expire.

1812
John Adams writes to his old friend Thomas Jefferson after years of not speaking to him. They renew their friendship, writing many letters to each other for the next 14 years.

1818
John Adams feels great sorrow when Abigail, his wife of 54 years, dies.

1824
John Quincy Adams, son of John and Abigail Adams, is elected president.

1826
On July 4, at nearly 91 years of age, John Adams dies on the 50th anniversary of the Declaration of Independence. Thomas Jefferson dies on the same day, just hours before.

GLOSSARY

alien (AY-lee-un) An alien is a person who is not a citizen of the country where he or she lives. Congress proposed the Alien Acts to keep the country safe from foreign spies.

bill (BILL) A bill is an idea for a law presented to a group of lawmakers. Congress and the president decide if bills will become laws.

bribe (BRYB) A bribe is a reward (such as money) given to people in exchange for their agreeing to do something. French officials refused to see diplomats from the United States unless the Americans paid a bribe.

cabinet (KAB-eh-net) A cabinet is the group of people who advise a president. John Adams kept the cabinet members that George Washington had chosen.

constitution (kon-stih-TOO-shun) A constitution is the set of rules that a government has to follow. Adams wrote a new constitution for the state of Massachusetts.

Constitutional Convention (kon-stih-TOO-shuh-nul kun-VEN-shun) The Constitutional Convention was the meeting where the U.S. Constitution was written. John Adams's book inspired the men who attended the Constitutional Convention.

Continental Congress (kon-tih-NEN-tul KONG-gris) The Continental Congress was the group of men who governed the United States during and after the Revolution. John Adams was a member of the Continental Congress.

deacon (DEE-kun) A deacon is a leader of a church. Deacons help ministers run a church.

democracy (deh-MOK-ruh-see) A democracy is a country in which citizens can vote and help run the government. The United States is a democracy.

Democratic-Republicans (deh-moh-KRAT-ik ree-PUB-lih-kenz) Democratic-Republicans were people who belonged to the Democratic-Republican Party, also known as the Republican Party. Democratic-Republicans thought states should keep a lot of power.

diplomat (DIP-luh-mat) A diplomat is a government official whose job is to represent a country in discussions with other countries. John Adams was a diplomat.

Electoral College (ee-LEKT-uh-rul KOL-ij) The Electoral College is made up of representatives from each state who vote for candidates in presidential elections. Members of the Electoral College cast their votes based on which candidate most people in their state prefer.

federal (FED-ur-ul) Federal means having to do with the central government of the United States, rather than a state or city government. Federalists believed that the U.S. federal government should have control over the states.

Federalists (FED-ur-ul-ists) Federalists were people who belonged to the Federalist Party, a political party in Adams's time. Federalists believed that the nation needed a strong central government.

foreign affairs (FOR-un uh-FAIRZ) Foreign affairs are matters involving other (foreign) countries. The president has to deal with foreign affairs, as well as problems at home.

immigrants (IM-uh-grentz) Immigrants are people who move from their homeland to a new country. Part of the Alien and Sedition Acts increased the length of time it took for immigrants to become U.S. citizens.

inauguration (ih-naw-gyuh-RAY-shun) An inauguration is the ceremony that takes place when a new president begins a term. John Adams administered the oath of office to George Washington at Washington's inauguration.

inheritance (in-HAYR-uh-tents) An inheritance is something one person leaves to another when he or she dies. John Adams received an inheritance from his father.

legislature (LEJ-uh-slay-chur) A legislature is a group of people elected to make laws. John Adams was elected to the Massachusetts legislature.

minister (MIN-uh-stur) A minister is a person who represents one country in another country. Adams was the U.S. minister to Great Britain.

monarchy (MON-ar-kee) A monarchy is a government run by a monarch, such as a king or a queen. Great Britain is a monarchy.

negotiate (neh-GOH-she-ayt) If people negotiate, they talk things over and try to come to an agreement. John Adams helped negotiate a treaty between the United States and England.

neutral (NOO-trul) If a country is neutral, it does not take sides during a war. George Washington believed the United States should remain neutral, rather than take sides in European wars.

nominate (NOM-uh-nayt) If a political party nominates someone, it chooses him or her to run for a political office. The Federalist Party nominated John Adams as its presidential candidate.

policies (PAWL-uh-seez) Policies are rules made to help run a government or other organization. The founding fathers created policies for the new country.

political parties (poh-LIT-uh-kul PAR-teez) Political parties are groups of people who share similar ideas about how to run a government. Today the two major U.S. political parties are the Democratic and Republican parties.

politics (PAWL-uh-tiks) Politics refers to the actions and practices of the government. As a young man, John Adams wrote about politics.

preside (preh-ZYD) If someone presides over a meeting, he or she is in charge of it and must keep order during discussions. Vice President Adams presided over the Senate.

representatives (rep-ree-ZEN-tuh-tivz) Representatives are people who attend a meeting, having agreed to speak or act for others. Congress is made up of representatives elected by the American people.

revolution (rev-uh-LOO-shun) A revolution is something that causes a complete change in government. The American Revolution was a war fought between the United States and England.

sedition (suh-DIH-shun) Sedition is something said or written, such as a newspaper article, that causes people to rebel against their government. American officials feared sedition during John Adams's presidency.

spokesperson (SPOHKS-pur-son) A spokesperson is one person who speaks for a group. Adams became a spokesperson for the patriots.

surrender (suh-REN-dur) If an army surrenders, it gives up to the enemy. When British General Cornwallis surrendered, he promised his soldiers would no longer fight the Americans.

treaty (TREE-tee) A treaty is a formal agreement made between nations. The United States and England signed a peace treaty after the American Revolution ended.

tutor (TOO-tur) To tutor is to give private lessons to someone. A lawyer agreed to tutor John Adams so he could learn about law.

THE UNITED STATES GOVERNMENT

The United States government is divided into three equal branches: the executive, the legislative, and the judicial. This division helps prevent abuses of power because each branch has to answer to the other two. No one branch can become too powerful.

EXECUTIVE BRANCH

PRESIDENT
VICE PRESIDENT
DEPARTMENTS

The job of the executive branch is to enforce the laws. It is headed by the president, who serves as the spokesperson for the United States around the world. The president signs bills into law and appoints important officials such as federal judges. He or she is also the commander in chief of the U.S. military. The president is assisted by the vice president, who takes over if the president dies or cannot carry out the duties of the office.

The executive branch also includes various departments, each focused on a specific topic. They include the Defense Department, the Justice Department, and the Agriculture Department. The department heads, along with other officials such as the vice president, serve as the president's closest advisers, called the cabinet.

LEGISLATIVE BRANCH

CONGRESS
Senate and
House of Representatives

The job of the legislative branch is to make the laws. It consists of Congress, which is divided into two parts: the Senate and the House of Representatives. The Senate has 100 members, and the House of Representatives has 435 members. Each state has two senators. The number of representatives a state has varies depending on the state's population.

Besides making laws, Congress also passes budgets and enacts taxes. In addition, it is responsible for declaring war, maintaining the military, and regulating trade with other countries.

JUDICIAL BRANCH

SUPREME COURT
COURTS OF APPEALS
DISTRICT COURTS

The job of the judicial branch is to interpret the laws. It consists of the nation's federal courts. Trials are held in district courts. During trials, judges must decide what laws mean and how they apply. Courts of appeals review the decisions made in district courts.

The nation's highest court is the Supreme Court. If someone disagrees with a court of appeals ruling, he or she can ask the Supreme Court to review it. The Supreme Court may refuse. The Supreme Court makes sure that decisions and laws do not violate the Constitution.

CHOOSING THE PRESIDENT

It may seem odd, but American voters don't elect the president directly. Instead, the president is chosen using what is called the Electoral College.

Each state gets as many votes in the Electoral College as its combined total of senators and representatives in Congress. For example, Iowa has two senators and five representatives, so it gets seven electoral votes. Although the District of Columbia does not have any voting members in Congress, it gets three electoral votes. Usually, the candidate who wins the most votes in any given state receives all of that state's electoral votes.

To become president, a candidate must get more than half of the Electoral College votes. There are a total of 538 votes in the Electoral College, so a candidate needs 270 votes to win. If nobody receives 270 Electoral College votes, the House of Representatives chooses the president.

With the Electoral College system, the person who receives the most votes nationwide does not always receive the most electoral votes. This happened most recently in 2000, when Al Gore received half a million more national votes than George W. Bush. Bush became president because he had more Electoral College votes.

THE WHITE HOUSE

The White House is the official home of the president of the United States. It is located at 1600 Pennsylvania Avenue NW in Washington, D.C. In 1792, a contest was held to select the architect who would design the president's home. James Hoban won. Construction took eight years.

The first president, George Washington, never lived in the White House. The second president, John Adams, moved into the house in 1800, though the inside was not yet complete. During the War of 1812, British soldiers burned down much of the White House. It was rebuilt several years later.

The White House was changed through the years. Porches were added, and President Theodore Roosevelt added the West Wing. President William Taft changed the shape of the presidential office, making it into the famous Oval Office. While Harry Truman was president, the old house was discovered to be structurally weak. All the walls were reinforced with steel, and the rooms were rebuilt.

Today, the White House has 132 rooms (including 35 bathrooms), 28 fireplaces, and 3 elevators. It takes 570 gallons of paint to cover the outside of the six-story building. The White House provides the president with many ways to relax. It includes a putting green, a jogging track, a swimming pool, a tennis court, and beautifully landscaped gardens. The White House also has a movie theater, a billiard room, and a one-lane bowling alley.

PRESIDENTIAL PERKS

The job of president of the United States is challenging. It is probably one of the most stressful jobs in the world. Because of this, presidents are paid well, though not nearly as well as the leaders of large corporations. In 2007, the president earned $400,000 a year. Presidents also receive extra benefits that make the demanding job a little more appealing.

★ **Camp David:** In the 1940s, President Franklin D. Roosevelt chose this heavily wooded spot in the mountains of Maryland to be the presidential retreat, where presidents can relax. Even though it is a retreat, world business is conducted there. Most famously, President Jimmy Carter met with Middle Eastern leaders at Camp David in 1978. The result was a peace agreement between Israel and Egypt.

★ *Air Force One*: The president flies on a jet called *Air Force One*. It is a Boeing 747-200B that has been modified to meet the president's needs.

Air Force One is the size of a large home. It is equipped with a dining room, sleeping quarters, a conference room, and office space. It also has two kitchens that can provide food for up to 50 people.

★ **The Secret Service:** While not the most glamorous of the president's perks, the Secret Service is one of the most important. The Secret Service is a group of highly trained agents who protect the president and the president's family.

★ **The Presidential State Car:** The presidential limousine is a stretch Cadillac DTS.

It has been armored to protect the president in case of attack. Inside the plush car are a foldaway desk, an entertainment center, and a communications console.

★ **The Food:** The White House has five chefs who will make any food the president wants. The White House also has an extensive wine collection.

★ **Retirement:** A former president receives a pension, or retirement pay, of just under $180,000 a year. Former presidents also receive Secret Service protection for the rest of their lives.

F A C T S

QUALIFICATIONS

To run for president, a candidate must

★ be at least 35 years old
★ be a citizen who was born in the United States
★ have lived in the United States for 14 years

TERM OF OFFICE

A president's term of office is four years.
No president can stay in office for more than two terms.

ELECTION DATE

The presidential election takes place every four years on the first Tuesday of November.

INAUGURATION DATE

Presidents are inaugurated on January 20.

OATH OF OFFICE

I do solemnly swear I will faithfully execute the office of the President of the United States and will to the best of my ability preserve, protect, and defend the Constitution of the United States.

WRITE A LETTER TO THE PRESIDENT

One of the best things about being a U.S. citizen is that Americans get to participate in their government. They can speak out if they feel government leaders aren't doing their jobs. They can also praise leaders who are going the extra mile. Do you have something you'd like the president to do? Should the president worry more about the environment and encourage people to recycle? Should the government spend more money on our schools? You can write a letter to the president to say how you feel!

1600 Pennsylvania Avenue
Washington, D.C. 20500
You can even send an e-mail to: president@whitehouse.gov

BOOKS

Collard, Sneed B., *John Adams: Our Second President.* New York: Marshall Cavendish Benchmark Books, 2006.

Feinberg, Barbara Silberdick. *John Adams.* New York: Children's Press, 2003.

Feinberg, Barbara Silberdick. *Next in Line: The American Vice Presidency.* New York: Franklin Watts, 1996.

Sutcliffe, Jane. *Abigail Adams.* Minneapolis: Lerner Publishers, 2006.

Sutcliffe, Jane. *John Adams.* Minneapolis: Lerner Publishers, 2006.

VIDEOS

The American President. DVD, VHS (Alexandria, VA: PBS Home Video, 2000).

The Declaration of Independence. DVD, VHS (Thousand Oaks, CA: Goldhil Video, 2000).

Founding Brothers. DVD, VHS (New York: The History Channel, 2002).

The History Channel Presents The Presidents. DVD (New York: A & E Home Video, 2005).

John and Abigail Adams. DVD (Alexandria VA: PBS Home Video, 2006).

National Geographic's Inside the White House. DVD (Washington, D.C.: National Geographic Video, 2003).

INTERNET SITES

Visit our Web page for lots of links about John Adams and other U.S. presidents:

http://www.childsworld.com/links

Note to Parents, Teachers, and Librarians: We routinely verify our Web links to make sure they are safe, active sites—so encourage your readers to check them out!

INDEX